ISBN: 0-9759580-0-3
Library of Congress
Cataloging-in-Publication Data available.

Published by Chicago Children's Museum
700 East Grand Avenue
Chicago, Illinois 60611
(312) 527-1000

www.ChiChildrensMuseum.org

Printed in Hong Kong.
Distributed by Independent Publishers Group.

THE skin YOU LIVE IN

written by MICHAEL TYLER

illustrated by DAVID LEE CSICSKO

CHICAGO CHILDREN'S MUSEUM

The wonderful skin you live in!

The skin you're all day in;
the skin that you play in;
the skin that you snuggle up,
cuddle up,
lay in...

The skin that you beam in;
the skin that you scream in;
the skin that you dream
about eating
ice cream in.

The skin you have fun in;
the skin that you run in;
the skin that you hop,
skip and jump in the sun in...

The skin you laugh in;
the skin that you cry in;
the skin that you look to
the sky and ask, "Why?" in.

It's baby born new skin and your family too skin, and glows when it shows that it knows we love you skin!

It's face the rain bold skin
and snow-angel cold skin,
and warm again,
let it in,
sunshine behold skin!

It's trembling fright skin
and cringes at night skin,
but turn off the lights
to make birthday-cake
bright skin.

It's whatever you do skin,
be happy it's you skin.
You can't live without it---
I'm glad it's me
too skin!

And look
at the shades
it comes in---
the shades of your
colorful skin!

Your coffee
and cream skin,
your warm cocoa
dream skin...

Your chocolate
chip, double
dip sundae
supreme skin!

Your marshmallow treat skin, your spun sugar sweet skin... your cherry topped, candy dropped, frosting complete skin.

Your pumpkin pie slice skin,
your caramel corn nice skin;
your toffee wrapped,
ginger snapped,
cinnamon spice skin!

Your butterscotch gold skin,
your lemon tart bold skin;
your mountain high apple pie,
cookie dough rolled skin!

Now, look once again at your skin...

And the skin all
people live in!

It's not tall skin
or short skin,
or best in the sport skin;
or fat skin or thin skin,
you lose and I win skin…

Nor sad skin
or mad skin,
you're naturally
bad skin;
I'm rich and you're poor
and you'll never have more skin.

It's not dumb skin or smart skin,
or keep us apart skin;
or weak skin or strong skin,
I'm right and you're wrong skin.

Nor she skin or he skin,
you're better than me skin;
I'm lesser than you skin,
it's me against you skin.

It's not any of this,

'cause you're more

than you seem.

You are all that you think and you hope and you dream.

You're a gifted
creation
with imagination.
You're a
new day desire
to reach
even higher.

You're the feelings that start,
from down deep in your heart.
You're the pride and the joy
inside each girl and boy.

So whenever you look
at your beautiful skin,
from your wiggling toes
to your giggling grin...

Think how lucky you are
that the skin you live in,
so beautifully holds the
"You" who's within.

And like flowers in the fields
that make wonderful views,
when we stand side-by-side
in our wonderful hues...

We all make a beauty,
so wonderfully true.
We are special and different
and just the same, too!

ACKNOWLEDGEMENTS

I express tremendous gratitude to my son, Sascha, for having inspired this poem; my wife, Julie, for always being there; the brilliance of David Lee Csicsko; the incredible Marcie Roman; everyone at Chicago Children's Museum and most importantly to "Giggles Twinkletoes," without whom this book would have never been.

MICHAEL TYLER, author

Drawing and designing this book was an absolute delight. Special thanks go to my great pals David Syrek, Tom Bachtell and Steve Musgrave. Also many thanks to Peter Szollosi who led me to this project and Randi Fiat for her endless encouragement and extra groovy big thanks to Kevin Putz for his help on the book and getting me to the finish line!

DAVID LEE CSICSKO, illustrator

CHICAGO CHILDREN'S MUSEUM

Chicago Children's Museum is the place where play and learning connect!

Located on historic Navy Pier, Chicago Children's Museum (CCM) presents lively learning adventures to kids through age 10 and their families, and celebrates the rich, cultural diversity that defines Chicago.

Only at CCM can visitors dig for bones in a *Dinosaur Expedition*, create a big splash in *WaterWays*, scale a towering schooner, learn to dance the *bhangra*, or make a Puerto Rican *jibarito* mask in a real, working art studio. With three floors of hands-on exhibits, daily programs and multicultural performances, CCM is the only museum in.Chicago dedicated exclusively to young children and one of the premier institutions of its kind in the country.

www.ChiChildrensMuseum.org

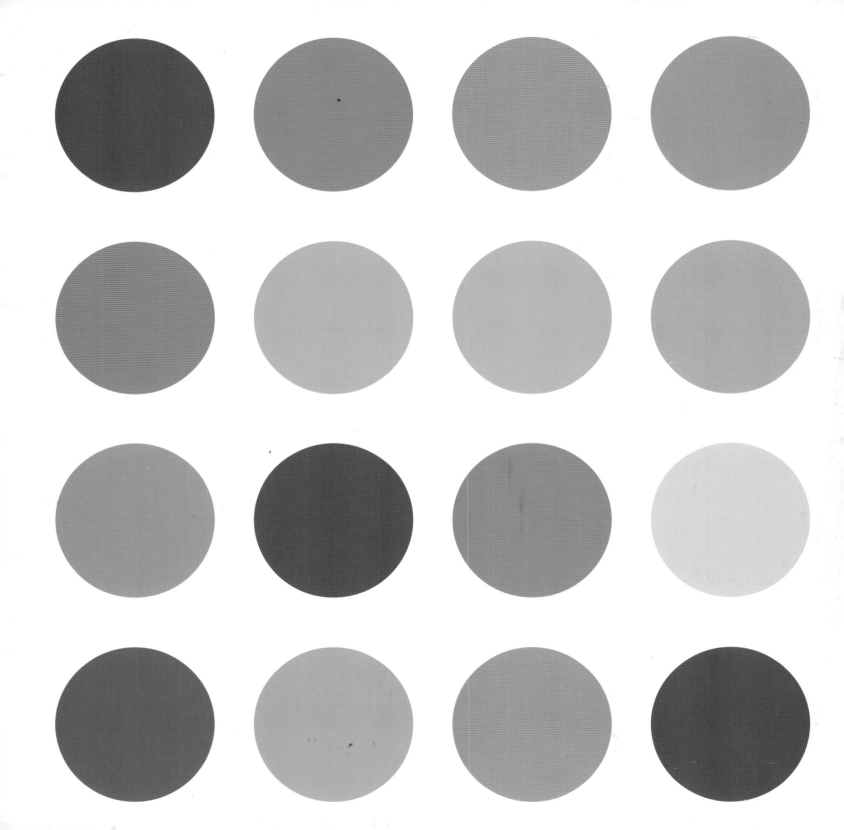